Bruges & Antwerp Travel Guide

Attractions, Eating, Drinking, Shopping & Places To Stay

James Benson

If there are any errors or omissions in copyright acknowledgements the publisher will be pleased to insert the appropriate acknowledgement in any subsequent printing of this publication.

Although we have taken all reasonable care in researching this book we make no warranty about the accuracy or completeness of its content and disclaim all liability arising from its use

Table of Contents

Bruges

Bruges' picture postcard image has been attracting visitors for hundreds of years. The Belgian city's gentle canals, narrow streets and fairy-tale rooftops appear lost in time. Romantic at anytime of the year, Bruges is a small city that can be easily explored on foot.

Bruges attracts visitors from all corners of the globe and is one of Belgium's most visited cities. Bruges (Brugge in Flemish) is generally free from the shoulder to shoulder hoards that descend on many of Europe's big hitters, allowing tourists to roam the winding canals that intertwine with the medieval architecture the city is famous for.

Bruges history dates back to 2000 years ago, with the earlier settlers trading with England, and later with Scandinavia, before eventually becoming a commercial centre for Europe in the 11th century due to its ideal, centralized location. Cloth and woolen goods became Bruges niche, with buyers from all corners of Europe doing trade with the Flemish city, and by 14th and 15th centuries Bruges population was twice that of the current population today, and very few European cities could match its wealth.

The city went through many highs and lows in the centuries that followed, with the difference in wealth between the rich and the poor becoming a common reason for revolts against the leaders. Art however, continued to flourish, and to this day - along with Bruges monuments, museums, and the world-renowned preservation of the cities buildings and streets - continues to attract visitors.

It is this preservation which occasionally sparks debate amongst historians and local folk. While it is clear that the city takes great pride in the appearance of its building, streets and canals, Bruges has gone through dozens of renovations of the centuries, something necessary in order to preserve its 13th century charm, and to give visitors an insight into the city's past. While the buildings and cobbled streets certainly do retain the city's old medieval appearance, most of this work is from the 19th and 20th centuries.

Culture

With an easily navigable city, Bruges can easily be explored on foot, however during the summer high season the locals like to take a bike and head out to the surrounding countryside and green spaces to kick back, and it's kicking back and enjoying life is what the people of Bruges are raised to do. Many of life's greatest treats and luxuries form the forefront of Bruges culture, including chocolate, beer, art, and jewelry.

The city has dozens of chocolatiers for those with a sweet tooth, while the sheer choice of beer options from bar to bar is overwhelming even for the expert. The city's arts scene is spread out across 30 museums, while the local jewellers are frequented by visitors from all over Europe looking to seal that quality piece for a special occasion.

Away from the culture of the good life, the city has become a photographer's dream, with novices and professionals constantly setting up their tripods around the city to catch the summer sun glazing over the soothing canals, or the snowcapped, fairytale rooftops that pierce the sky during the festive period.

In 2000, Bruges was recognized as UNESCO World Heritage Site, before being named European Capital of Culture in 2003, injecting millions of euros into the city and enabling the preservations and up keeping of the city to flourish.

Bruges architecture is firmly embedded into the history of the city, with different buildings highlight the contrasting stages of the city's development, ranging from an early brick gothic, to the later neo-Gothic style of which both are now so fondly associated with the city of Bruges.

Location & Orientation

Situated in the northwest of the country, Bruges is the capital and largest city of the Belgian province of Flanders, just 39km from Ghent, 83km from Antwerp and 90km from the countries capital Brussels. The city is also located just 13km to the sea, which can be a popular getaway during the summer time, or almost year round for surfers looking to catch a wave.

The city itself is divided into five neighbourhoods. Markt and Burg, which is the centre of the city and encompasses the main square; Minnewater-Astrid Park, which is a residential area located within easy walking distance of the centre, and is dotted with small parks; St. Anna, names after St. Anna church which sits in the centred of this cobblestoned area of town; and St, Giles, known as the quieter part of town, and located on the other side of the canal.

Climate & When to Visit

While Bruges does get four unique seasons, the extremities of these seasons are rare, making the city a good option for tourists all year round.

Spring is the most popular time to visit, with highs averaging between 11°C and 22°C. Summer is certainly the most popular time to visit, and although the city can seem crowded, the city doesn't get too crowded or too hot like many of Europe's other major draws, allowing tourists a more comfortable experience whilst still being able to enjoy the summer sun. Highs of 24°C are normal, and a plethora of outdoor activities and cultural events are guaranteed to be taking place during the months of and August.

The autumn is without doubt the quietest time of year, with the city winding down after the summer, and if caught on a nice clear crisp day, the city can make for a memorable visit with you almost having the city to yourself amongst the colours and (rare) sunshine the season can produce.

Most of the winter is Bruges is just as quiet, although the Christmas winter markets normally put an end to the desertedness throughout the month of December. And while temperatures hover between -1°C and 6°C, this time of year can certainly be a romantic time, particularly if you are lucky to catch the city after a sprinkling of snow.

Sightseeing Highlights

The Markt

Located in the very centre of the city, The Markt – also known as the Market Square – has been used as a Market Place since the tenth century, and still operates the same weekly haggle-fest every Wednesday when locals and tourists come together to negotiate over handicrafts, clothes, food, and all things Flemish. The Markt is surrounded by some of the city's most impressive architecture, including the towering Belfry alongside the Cloth Hall to the north and the Bruges Post Office to the east. The rest of the square is dotted trendy restaurants and chic cafes, making the Market Square an ideal meeting place for both tourists and locals.

At the centre of the square stand's the statues of Jan Breydel and Pieter de Coninck, two instrumental leaders during the war with the French in 1302. At night, the square is classic continental Europe at its most romantic. Couples adorn the squares benches while the lights twinkle against the looming, neo-gothic monuments. A summer evening relaxing on one of the outdoor terraces can be as relaxing and romantic as you imagine a European city to be, however it is advisable to choose wisely, as some of the restaurants and bars surrounding the Market Square can be very expensive although there are also reasonable options.

The Belfry

Towering over the city of Bruges at 83 metres tall, the Belfry is one of Bruges must see attractions and offers by far and out the best vista in Bruges, and possible within Belgium. First and foremost however, a climb of 366 steps is required to reach the top, taking in narrow, winding staircases which can be a little cramped in parts.

The climb isn't a total grind, however. En-route, tourists can enjoy the sounds of the towers carillion, which consists of 46 bells, whilst exploring the treasury as well as the extraordinary clockwork mechanism. Once a few rest stops have been taken, the final ascent compensates visitors with a stunning view of the whole city and its surrounding countryside. On a clear day, or even during the early winter darkness – the tower closes at 5:00pm - tourists normally spend some time at the top enjoying the distant views.

The Belfry is a medieval bell tower also known as the Belfort, and being located in the Market Square, is more or less right in the centre of the city. Possibly Bruges' most striking icon, the Belfry used to be home to a treasury, and was also used as a lookout point for identifying hazards or unusual activities in and around the city, with the bells each having a different sound to notify the city of danger, announcements and more frequently, the time.

The tower was originally ravaged by a fire in 1280, and has been rebuilt numerous times over the centuries, but it still retains its gothic feel. Today it is the 17th century charm which attracts many visitors annually.

The Belfry of Bruges
Markt 7,
8000 Brugge,
Belgium
Tel.: 050 44 87 67

Open: every day from 9:30am until 5:00pm.
Price: €5 Adults; Free entrance for children under 13 years of age.

The Burg

The Burg is a second, smaller public square situated just seconds away from the Markt, and houses its own display of fine buildings, each giving their own piece of history to the city. In was here where the fortified castle, known as a 'burg' was built to protect the village which went on to become the city Bruges.

The Old Town Hall – which dates back to the 1300's - is one of the most impressive buildings in the city and is located within this square. To the right of the Old Town Hall is the Old Civil Registry, which was finished in 1537, but underwent a restoration itself in the late 18th century after its adorning statues – which symbolize Justice, Moses and Aaron - were ruined.

For first time visitors, the best and most romantic way to approach the Burg is from the cobbled street of the same name, passing under the arch at the Old Civil Registry and across a pretty little bridge. Couples and families alike stroll through this scenic walkway taking in the pleasant surroundings before reaching the square with its looming architecture

The Church of Our Lady

Taking two centuries to complete and rising to 122 metres, the Church of Our Lady was built in the 15th century and is home to a wealth of artistic gems and attracts tourists for its impressive collection as well as its commanding presence upon the skyline of the city. The church possesses the only piece of art from Renaissance sculptor Michelangelo that left Italy during his life, and is today one of his few pieces that can be viewed outside of his home country – a marble statue carved in 1504 representing Madonna and Child.

The church also houses Anthony van Dyck's painting of the Crucifixion of Christ, Pieter Poubus' Last Supper and Adoration of the Shepherds and Gerard
David's Transfigeration, whilst dominating the choir isle are the striking, juxtaposing bronze tomb statues of the Duke of Burgundy Charles the Bold, and his young daughter Mary who, being a keen rider, died at just 25 years old when she fell off her horse.
The Duke died in battle in France.

The Church of Our Lady
Mariastraat 38
8000 Brugge,
Belgium
Tel.: 050 34 53 14
Web: www.onthaalkerk-brugge.be

Basilica of the Holy Blood

The Basilica of the Holy Blood is a 12th century Roman Catholic Church, and is most famous for the relic that is housed inside, which is said to contain the blood of Jesus Christ. The relic – a piece of bloodstained cloth –was said to be collected by Joseph of Arimathea after the crucifixion, and brought to Bruges from the Kingdom of Israel. The church was built between 1134 and 1157.

Situated in the Burg square, the basilica has a lower and upper chapel, with the upper chapel housing the treasured relic. The lower chapel was built as a testament to St. Basil the Great, and except for some renovations during the 1500's, remains largely unmodified.

The relic can be viewed by the public every Friday.

Basilica of the Holy Blood
Burg 13,
8000 Brugge,
Belgium
Tel.: 050 33 67 92

Renaissance Hall of the Palace of Liberty

The Renaissance Hall is housed inside the Palace of Liberty, and is a 15th century room – the only surviving room from the original building – which displays outstanding examples of Renaissance art from the 15th and 16th centuries. Known in Bruges as the Renaissancezaal 't Brugse Vrije, the room is led by the huge marble and oak chimneypiece which was carved to ceremonialize the triumph over the French in 1525.

The Palace of Liberty - with the Liberty being the district that surrounded Bruges in the 10th century – dates back to 1722 after it was built to replace a 16th century mansion of which the now known Renaissance Hall was originally housed.

The palace was built to be the seat of the Liberty of Bruges, before being used as a courthouse over 100 years later.

Today, the palace is home to the Bruges Council, and inside the Renaissance Hall has been restored to its past self, with its original and grand black marble fireplace still in place.

The Palace of the Liberty of Bruges
Burg 11
8000 Brugge,
Belgium
Tel.: 050 44 87 11
Opening time: Daily 9.30am–12.30pm & 1.30–5pmPrice: €2.50.

St. John's Hospital & Museum

Standing opposite the Church of Lady, St. Johns Hospital - known locally as Sint-Janshospitaal - is one of Europe's oldest preserved hospitals, and takes visitors on a trip to the 12th century onwards, getting an up close and personal view of how healthcare was back in the middle ages, right up until 1978 when the building no longer functioned as a place of care.

Now a museum, the hospital still contains medical apparatus in the original hospital wards, while 13th century paintings give an accurate image of the hospital during its operational days.

As the museum educates visitors more about latter hospital life, giving examples of how the wards, beds and other facilities would have looked then, typical furniture, paintings, and sculptures line the hallways and waiting rooms, exemplifying the hospitals powerful and wealthy status.

The oldest part of the building was built around the 12th century, and was primarily used to offer shelter and care for emigrants, and visiting businessmen. Originally, those with minor illnesses were allowed, whilst those with contagious or mental sicknesses were always declined, as the hospital during its early centuries could only offer people shelter, a little food and religious assistance during their final moments.

As the years went by, the hospital developed and even expanded rapidly to accommodate the growth of the city, and eventually became a fully functioning hospital until the late 1970's. During this decade the city of Bruges decided a newer, more modern building would be needed, and St. John's Hospital soon became a museum to display its long and successful past.

Sint-Janshospitaal
Mariastraat 38,
8000 Brugge,
Belgium
Tel.: 050 44 87 71
Hours: Tuesday until Sunday, 9:00am until 5:00pm; closed Mondays.

Groeninge Museum

The Groeninge Museum – also referred to as the city museum of Fine Arts – houses an impressive collection of Flemish and Belgian paintings spanning across six centuries. Whilst the collection has been steadily expanding since the early 1700s, the building itself was not built until 1930. Named after the Groeninge fields - where victory over the French was competed in 1302 – the museums striking collection is generally prioritized on pieces by painters who were born and plied their trade in the city, with Bruges local Jan van Eyck receiving significant exposure, as well as works by famous names including Hans Memling, Rogier van der Weyden and Hieronymus Bosch.

The Groeninge Museum,
Dijver 12
8000 Brugge,
Belgium
Tel.: 050 44 87 51
Open hours: Tuesday to Sunday from 9:30am until 5:00pm.
Price: Adults €8; 6-25 years €1; 0-5 years free.

The Arentshuis

The Arentshuis is a smaller museum connected to the Groeninge Museum, and is located in an exquisite 18th century dwelling and flanked by one of Bruges' most charming gardens. The gardens themselves are handsomely stocked with outdoor pieces of art including Rik Poot's Horsemen of the Apocalypse, four bronze statues representing pestilence, war, famine, and death, taken from the story from the Book of Revelation of Saint John the Evangelist, the last book from the New Testament. The gardens alone are worth a visit, and one can enjoy the surrounding while exploring many scattered pieces and monuments.

Temporary art exhibitions are held one the ground floor throughout the year, with many associated with the nearby Groeninge Museum, while the upper level is allotted to the impressive pieces of Bruges-born British artist, Frank Brangwyn, who produced buoyant and earthly paintings in which he characterized the lives of the local working class of the nearby ports. Brangwyn was also known for his unique designs of furniture, carpets, glasswork and jewelry.

The Arentshuis
Dijver 16,
8000 Brugge,
Belgium
Tel.: 050 44 87 63
Hours: Tuesday to Sunday, 9:30am until 5:00pm; Closed on Mondays.
Price: €3, or free with a ticket from the Groeninge Museum.

Gruuthuse Museum

Located in the Our Lady's Church, the Gruuthuse Museum is an extravagant palace of the Lords of Gruuthuse - one of the country's richest families, who resided here between the 1400s and 1800s – and through the extensive collection of art, furniture, tapestries and architecture, gives an insight into life as part of one of the wealthiest families during medieval times. The palace also includes a prayer chapel, which ensured the Lords of Gruuthuse express access to the Church of Our Lady.

The main hallway is lined with splendid tapestries, an eloquent fireplace, and handsomely finished wooden beams, all which only goes to certify the fortunes of the Lords of Gruuthuse. The most well known member of the family is Lodewijk van Gruuthuse, whose equestrian statue stands at the front of the Gruuthuse palace overlooking the lower level.

The Gruuthuse Museum
Dijver 17,
8000 Brugge,
Belgium
Tel.: 050 44 87 43
Web: www.museabrugge.be
Hours: Tuesday to Sunday, 9:30am until 5:00pm; closed Mondays.
Price: €6; €1 for ages 6-25; Free for residents of Bruges and Children under 6 years of age.

Recommendations for the Budget Traveller

Places to Stay

While Bruges is now regarded as Belgium's most popular destination for both local and foreign tourists, accommodation prices have yet to reach the highs set by the capital city of Brussels, who owe much of their heavy hotel prices to the influx of business and political visitors year round. The majority of Bruges' visitors are here for the sights, and the reasonable accommodation options coupled with the remarkably willing locals put the city up there with some of the continents best traveler friendly destinations.

As with most accommodation options in Europe, breakfast is included with many rates as standard, with lots of places offering heavy discounts for groups of up to four and five staying in the same room or suite. As Europe's backpacking trail continues to expand, more and more hostels are popping up in Bruges and the surrounding Flanders region.

As Bruges is a surprisingly small city, all accommodation quoted is located within the city limits, offering ease of access to the main attractions.

Snuffel Backpacker Hostels

Ezelstraat 47-49
8000 Brugge,
Belgium
Tel.: 050 33 31 33
Web: www.snuffel.be

Located in the charming old part of the city, the Snuffel Backpacker hostel is one of the most well-known places for backpackers to rest their heads, due to its array of free amenities and budget friendly prices. Some of these free amenities include a hearty breakfast every day, Wi-Fi, city discount card for most major attractions, parking, daily guided walking tours, and two free concerts every month with performances from local bands and artists.

The hostel also includes a modern and fully equipped kitchen, a library, bicycle store for rentals and storage, on site laundry and a tranquil patio area for guests to relax and enjoy one of the 25 beers to hostel offers on tap, in particular during the nightly happy hour.

Eight bed mixed dorms from €16 per person per night; four bed mixed dorm from €17 per person per night, with sheets included.

Bruges Budget Hotel

Langestraat 127-133,
8000 Brugge,
Belgium
Tel.: 050 34 10 93

The Bruges Budget Hotel is an ideal choice for couples and families, or for those who simply don't fancy the idea of sleeping in dormitory style accommodation. The hotels rates are remarkably low for a twin or double room, and with free breakfast and Wi-Fi as well as a complimentary walking tour four days per week, the Bruges Budget Hotel is one of the those rare steals to be found in a top European city. The hotels exterior has a romantic feel, set in a classical Brugean step gable house it typifies Bruges postcard image.

With an onsite Flemish restaurant and bar offering a choice of 450 beers and bicycle rental to explore the city, this hotel guarantees the perfect Flemish and Belgian experience without putting too much of a dent in your wallet.

The Bruges Budget Hotel offers double or twin rooms with private en-suite bathroom for just €25 per person per night.

Hotel Leopold

Hoogste van Brugge
8000 Brugge,
Belgium
Tel.: 050 33 51 29
Web: www.hotelleopold.be

Located in the pretty square of 'tZand, right in the centre of Medieval Bruges is the budget friendly Hotel Leopold, which offers ten clean and airy rooms in its small, family run hotel. Each room has its own individual design, and offers the perfect relaxing atmosphere for both families and couples. All rooms offer private facilities and amenities such as an en-suite bathroom and cable TV.

Upon entrance to the hotel via the romantic cobblestoned alleyway, guests can immediately turn to relaxation mode as the hotels friendly yet tranquil atmosphere ensures the perfect getaway. Breakfast is on the house, with an extensive array of cereals accompanied by a hot buffet style, continental breakfast. Wi-Fi connection is available for a small fee, which allows access for the remainder of the day or for the duration of your trip.

The Hotel Leopold offers rooms for two and four persons and depending on availability can accommodate up to six guests in one room if a request is made.

A double or twin room costs €35 per person per night, with standard four bed guest rooms costing €30 per person per night.

HI Europa Brugge

Baron Ruzettelaan 143
8310 Brugge,
Belgium
Tel.: 050 35 26 79
Web: www.hihostels.com

Part of the Hostelling International chain, which offers discount for its members, the HI Europa Brugge is set in a quiet part of the city and is perfect for those looking for an ideal location to explore Bruges, whilst at the same time having a nearby location to escape the hustle and bustle of the city centre. Set in its own relaxing grounds

The hostel is renowned for its generous and free breakfast, which is offered daily to guests to prepare for a day of exploring the cities nearby winding streets and canals, and the location is just minutes away from the centre of Bruges, and around a 10-15 minute walk to the main train station and transport hub. There are numerous convenience stores nearby offering snacks for a fraction of the price just streets away in the centre of town.

Once back on the grounds, guests can relax on the huge terrace area during a nice day, or spend a winter's day snuggled up in the relaxing TV room where travelers can generally mingle over a movie on one of the sprawling couches. The grounds also offer a bar and free Wi-Fi.

Six bed dorms cost from €18 per person per night with sheets included, with four bed dorms starting at €20 per person per night. Both options are available in male only and female only. Prices quoted are for those in possession of a Hostelling International or IYHF card. €3 will be added per person per night without this card. To obtain yours, see www.hihostels.com.

Jacobs Hotel Brugge

Baliestraat 1
8000 Brugge,
Belgium
Tel.: 050 33 98 31
Web: www.hoteljacobs.be

Centrally located in the heart of medieval Bruges, the Jacobs Hotel can be found on the street of Baliestraat, a quiet and charming street that lies in the shadows of the St. Gillis Cathedral, and just a stone's throw away from the Market Square. A hard combination to find in many European cities, the Jacobs Hotel is ideal for those looking to gain a little luxury out of their European city break, without breaking the bank, and all whilst staying centrally located.

Once guests can tear themselves away from the nearby picturesque streets and canals, the hotel – which was built in 1829 - offers a bar and restaurant, as well as authentic Belgian chocolates, combining the style and architecture of yesterday with all the modern facilities and amenities you could wish for. A full complimentary breakfast is included in all rates, and all rooms come with private amenities such as showering facilities, hairdryer, and cable television.

Rates begin at €33 per person per night in a family room of five, with double and twin rooms costing €39 per person per night. The hotel also offers three and four bed rooms, from €39 and €37 per person per night respectively, and all rooms come with a private en-suite bathroom.

Places to Eat

For those on a budget, there are many gems to be unearthed in the city of Bruges, however there are many rules and things to know in order to avoid falling into any of the classic tourist traps. Restaurants dotted around the Markt and the Burg squares are generally overpriced, and seemingly just exist to provide visitors with that European romantic fairy tale feeling while sitting on the patio surrounded by the architecture of yesteryear. While not all, many of these restaurants charge an extortionate price for the seemingly free bread and water, so it is wise to check if splurging on one of the more romantically placed restaurants.

The following however, are some of Bruges best budget eateries that can assure you there will be no sneaky €6 charge for a small bottle of water.

Brasserie Medard

Sint-Amandsstraat 18
8000 Brugge,
Belgium
Tel.: 050 34 86 84

Aimed at the easy going traveler looking for a dirt cheap sit down meal, Brasserie Medard ticks all the boxes for budget travelers – and that's before we even talk about the portion sizes. The brasserie is located in the centre of the city and just steps away from the Markt and Burg squares, the café style restaurant offers spaghetti meals for just €3-€4.

Typically, tourists pile in jostling for a spare table while locals are understandably given preferential treatment, but don't let this distract you. While most Flemish people are a little tough on the outside, this is highlighted by the family who run this charming restaurant that feels like its atmosphere is about to burst onto the street. Once you get their attention, the owners are extremely friendly and willing to share advice on the city as well as their own menu. On the other side of the coin, the restaurant can get a little hectic, however this only adds to the charm. The outdoor patio with tables and chairs is also laid out during the warmer months.

A selection of sandwiches for between €3 and €5, along with the renowned spaghetti which even those with the biggest appetites can struggle to complete, topped by a large, classic selection of Belgian beers ensure Bruges worst kept secret is ahead of the pack when it comes to not only grabbing a wholesome meal of great quality, but also for mixing with locals and fellow travelers alike.

Café Rose Red

Cordoeaniersstraat 16,
Bruges 8000,
Belgium
Tel.: 050 339 051
http://www.cordoeanier.be

Located inside the trendy Hotel Cordoeanier, again just a few steps from the main squares of the Markt and the Burg, it is difficult to believe from both the inviting exterior to the warm and cosy interior that this is a place for a few cheap bites, and while the food is primarily finger food, you can certainly purchase enough on shoestring to leave your hunger at bay while you take the selection of 120 beers – a more moderate and manageable amount by Belgian terms.

The calling card of this slick café will always be its beer, with a speciality in trappist beer, and this is what most punters are here for. It is however difficult to ignore the good food menu, and the café also offers a great breakfast. The café offers cheese boards and meat platters, as well as olives, with prices ranging from €2 to €5.

Open Monday to Thursday, 10:00am until 11:00pm; Friday and Saturday, 10:00am until 12:00am, and Sunday, 10:00am until 10:00pm.

Books & Brunch

30, Garenmarkt
Brugge, 8000
Belgium
Tel.: 050 70 90 79
Web: www.booksandbrunch.be

Fresh homemade food, centrally located, remarkably friendly staff, and of course, books. Books and Brunch is everything what their title promises – with a little more thrown in for good measure. Brunch is not the only time you can eat here as the restaurant also does and excellent breakfast and lunch either side, with breakfasts orders beginning at 8:30pm during weekdays.

The menu offers organic food as well as numerous vegetarian options, and visitors from all walks of life mix with locals over an extremely reasonably priced meal. The bistro style restaurant also doubles as a second hand bookstore, and there is a wealth of reading materials filling the walls around the place. Books can be browsed before, during or after your meal for free, and can also be bought for a few euros. Many visitors also come in for a tea or coffee and a quick read, and this all adds to the restaurant's relaxed vibe.

Meals between €4 and €20.

Opening hours: Monday to Friday, 8:30am until 6.00pm; Saturday, 09:00am until 6:00pm; closed Sundays.

In't Nieuw Museum

Hooistraat 42
8000 Brugge,
Belgium
Tel.: 050 33 12 80
Web: www.resto.be

The restaurant inside the In'l Nieuw Museum is located just outside of the main tourist area of Bruges, but can easily be reached from the downtown hotels in ten minutes of walking. The restaurants interior has a quirky design while the pleasant and friendly staff members offer excellent service with a smile, ensuring visitors who take the stroll off the beaten path stay to enjoy a nice evening in the restaurant.

With the meats and other produce freshly grilled on the open barbeque, and the mixed grill of steak, chicken, pork, T-bone and sausage is highly recommended as well as the barbequed ribs.

The restaurant also offers some great mussels of which the city is becoming famous for. Dinner prices are more than reasonable for a European city, and this is topped with a wonderful atmosphere inside the restaurant.

Dinner prices from €20 per person.

Den Amand

Sint-Amandstraat 4,
Bruges 8000,
Belgium
Tel.: 050 34012
Web: www.denamand.be

For those looking to capture the scene of central Bruges over a romantic meal without breaking the bank at one of the restaurants that line the main squares, then the perfect answer is located just a two minute walk from the Markt and the Burg in the very centre of the city. You get the views of the buildings, and a small patio allows guest to soak up the European ambience.

The only difference with this restaurant is that not only is the price a fraction of what you would pay just seconds away, but the vibe received from the waiters, the wall art and the fellow diners was that of a true Flemish experience. Den Amand has a great Shrimp Linguine, as well as accommodating very well for vegetarians. The restaurant also has that trademark beer collection, with an impressive menu of beers to accommodate your meal.

Dinner mains start from €20 per person.

Places to Shop

L'Héroïne

Noordzandstraat 32
8000 Brugge,
Belgium
Tel.: 050 33 56 57
Web: www.lheroine.be

In the centre of Bruges lies a small boutique which offers nothing but items from the leading designers in Belgium. L'Héroïne, with its modern and artsy décor has a team of knowledgeable staff who will work with you to find the perfect garment, while offering experienced recommendations – all with a smile.

For those looking for something unique, and keeping their options within the country limits, L'Héroïne is the perfect choice.

Dijver

Europa College
8000 Dijver,
Bruges,
Belgium

Every Weekend outside the Europa College (College of Europe) opens up a huge Flea Market at the Dijver, which offers everything from handicrafts, souvenirs, and an array of clothing for all tastes.

Situated right on Den Dijver, one of the city's most scenic canals, the flea market is a haggler's paradise, with locals and tourists mixing amongst the isles and stalls which are doused in what would seem like an atmosphere that hasn't changed since the Middle Ages.

The stalls are set up right in front of the college and cannot be missed, and the market runs from 10:00am until 6:00pm, every Saturday and Sunday from March until mid-November.

Breidelstraat

Being the street that connects the two main squares of the Markt and the Burg, it was only a matter of time before Breidelstraat was lined with an array of shopping options down its narrow and shady street. Here are some of the city's best chocolatiers that line up alongside some surprisingly inexpensive souvenir shops. There are countless fashion options along the street, ranging from local designers to the well-known high street brands, giving a something for everybody feel as you walk along the street that is lined by some of Bruges most spectacular architecture.

Antwerp

Antwerp is the second largest city in Belgium with a population of 500,000 in the metropolitan area. Known as the "Daughter of the River Scheldt," Antwerp has a famous diamond industry but this Belgian city has many other attractions to interest its visitors.

Antwerp has the second largest harbour in Europe and this has historically brought an array of cultures and products to the city.

It is this grand harbour that at one time made the city one of the most influential in the world. When the Spanish took over the city in 1585, the city's influence was replaced by Amsterdam, and the city fell into a slump until the 19th century when economic growth began to return the city to its former splendor.

This economic growth is visible in many different areas around the city today. While the 15th century architecture is one attraction, the modern architecture and contemporary artistic influences brought by a changing economy are also a draw for travelers. With picturesque views of the old world meeting the new, you can be sure that Antwerp will shine like a diamond in your memories for years.

Culture

While today Antwerp is known for diamonds and less for its maritime past, the people of Antwerp are working to bring this culture to the forefront with a new harbour museum and other attractions.

Antwerp is also known for its fashion and art. In recent years, a number of well-known designers, actors, and artists have emerged from the city including Timo Descamps (actor), André Cluytens (conductor) and Ferre Grignard (singer/songwriter).

The Royal Ballet of Flanders also moved to a new space in Antwerp bringing more attention on the city.

The nightlife in Antwerp is vibrant and it is home to more than 2,000 bars and clubs. Coupled with the more than 700 distinct beers that are brewed in Belgium, it is the perfect location for the beer enthusiast. In fact some say that Belgian beers are the best in the world. You'll have to investigate that for yourself!

The people of Antwerp speak their own dialect of Dutch called Antverpian. While similar to other Dutch dialects, it is distinctive by its very specific vowel pronunciations. Do not worry though! With all of the tourism and trade, it is easy to find locals who speak English, Spanish, French, and a host of other languages.

Location & Orientation

Antwerp (Antwerpen as the locals call it) is located in the Flanders region of Northern Belgium. The metropolitan area rests on the border of Belgium and Netherlands and some of the suburbs of Antwerp are actually located in both countries.

The main part of the city is settled on the eastern bank of the Scheldt River where it begins to narrow as it moves inland. Antwerp fans out around its large harbour, and although the harbour is constructed on both sides of the river, the west bank is not considered to be a part of the Metropolis because it is in the province of East Flanders, not the Antwerp province.

The Antwerp metropolitan area is comprised of 22 neighborhoods. A few of the neighborhoods that are considered the most important are: 't Zuid (the South), Theaterbuurt (also called Quartier Latin), Antwerpen Noord (Old City, which includes Stuivenberg, Seefhoek, Amandus-Atheneum, and Chinatown), Centraal Station (which includes the areas of Kievitwijk, Diamant, Statiekwartier, Joods Antwerpen), and Historisch Centrum.

Antwerp can be reached through one of three airports. Antwerp Airport (ANR) is located in the city. Brussels Airport (BRU) is located only 26 miles (42km) from Antwerp. The largest airport is Schiphol Airport (AMS) in Amsterdam, which is roughly 100 miles (160 km) away.

Map of Antwerp attractions:
http://www.planetware.com/map/antwerp-map-b-ant_ce.htm

Climate & When to Visit

The climate of Antwerp is relatively cool year-round. In the winter months, the average temperature is around 6 degrees Celsius. In the summer months, the average temperature is 22 degrees Celsius, makings it the perfect place to relax without having to worry about getting too overheated.

As with many northern European cities, the best time to visit Antwerp is in the summer. The excellent summer weather means that the time for festivals is perfect. 'Zomer van Antwerpen,' or Summer in Antwerp, is a four month festival from July to October with many different cultural events, musical concerts, and theatrical productions.

Concerts and parades occur in the city during most weeks of the summer. Open-air concerts are extremely popular towards the end of July and the beginning of August. If fashion holds more interest for you, the Academy Fashion Show runs throughout June, giving every fashionista the opportunity to see work by up-and-coming designers fresh out of the Royal Antwerp Academy of Fine Arts.

Smaller festivals and cultural events happen year-round, making any time of year ideal for visiting. Antwerp is also a great place to go ice-skating, which is very popular in late December and throughout January.

Getting to Antwerp

Due to its central location between Brussels and Amsterdam, getting to Antwerp is easy in almost every mode of transportation. Buses come into Antwerp from most major cities and stop at the Franklin Rooseveltplaats Terminal, which is conveniently located near the Old City Centre. The two main bus lines in and out of the city are Eurolines and Ecolines (which runs out of Berchem Station Square).

The recently renovated Centraal Station has made train travel to Antwerp much easier for travelers. The two routes that will get you to Antwerp are the Amsterdam-Brussels train, ran by Belgian Railways, and the Amsterdam-Paris train, which is ran by Thalys. The first train runs roughly 1 hour 50 minutes from Amsterdam. The Thalys train, however, is a high-speed train, and takes about one hour. Tickets cost nearly twice as much to get a seat on the Thalys train and it can book up in advance.

The three airports that are within easy distance of Antwerp are Antwerp Airport, Brussels Airport, and Schiphol Airport. The first is Antwerp Airport (ANR). While it is wonderful to have an airport conveniently located just outside of the city center, ANR is only serviced by one airline: CityJet Airlines. Because of this there are only six flights in and out of the city each day. These flights go to London City Airport (LCY), Manchester (MAN), Dublin (DUB), Dundee (DND), Edinburgh (EDI), and Jersey (JER). However, because the airport is so conveniently located, bus and taxi fares to the city centre usually are under €10. Its location also makes it a big draw for those on business trips.

Brussels Airport (BRU) is the next closest airport to Antwerp. The short trip from Brussels Airport to Antwerp can be easily covered by the airport bus that leaves to and from the city once every hour. In Antwerp, the bus makes two stops, one at the city center and one at the Hotel Crowne Plaza. There is also a train that leaves once an hour, and conveniently arrives in the center of town at Centraal Station. This airport is perfect for the budget savvy traveler as airline tickets tend to be cheaper, and the cost of traveling to Antwerp is inexpensive.

Schiphol Airport (AMS) is the final airport within close proximity of Antwerp. Located in Amsterdam, this airport is nearly two hours from Antwerp. If you do not want to drive the option for getting to Antwerp is by train (as previously discussed). While the cost of tickets in and out of the airport are relatively low, the cost of travel to Antwerp makes this airport somewhat uninviting.

Sightseeing Highlights

Museum by the River (Museum aan de Stroom)

Hanze Stedenplaats 1 't Gilandje
Tel: 03 206 09 40
www.mas.be
Hours: Tuesday-Sunday 1000-1700

The Museum aan de Stroom is one of the newest museums in Antwerp, opening in 2011. The museum shows off the extensive history of the city.

The main themes covered in the museum are Power (electricity), the Metropolis, Life and Death in the city, and Port history.

While the history inside the museum is amazing, the architecture of the building is also quite a draw. The building is six stories tall and built with alternating patterns of Indian Stone and glass to give it an extremely modern look. It is also home to nearly 500,000 artifacts, although only about half of them are available to be viewed by the public.

To incorporate the modern feel of the building with the history of the artifacts, the museum uses QR codes on each display. If you want to learn more about the piece or the history behind it, you simply need to scan the code, and a multi-lingual website will pop up, giving you more information.

Plantin-Moretus Museum

Vrijdagmarkt 22 (Old City Centre)
Tel: 03 221 14 50
www.museumplantinmoretus.be
Adults: €6/concession: €4/children: free
Hours: Tuesday-Sunday: 1000-1700

In the 16th Century, Christophe Plantin started the world's first printing company. Since then, members of his family have worked in the printing business generation after generation. Today, the city of Antwerp has made this building into a museum honoring the history of print.

Along with the two oldest printing presses in the world, the Plantin-Moretus Museum contains many of some of the world's oldest printed works. For example, it is home to *Biblia Polyglotta* (1568), a Bible that was written in five languages. It is also home to paintings and drawings by Rubens, and studies by Justus Lipsius.

In 2005, the Plantin-Moretus Museum was added to the World Heritage Sites list, making it one of four such World Heritage Sites in Flanders. The museum also has its own history from World War II when a bomb was dropped on the building, destroying the south side (which has since been completely rebuilt).

Middelheim Open-Air Statuary Museum (Openluchtmuseum voor Beeldhouwkunst Middelheim)

Middelheim 61 (4 km south of Old City Centre)
Tel: 03 828 13 50
www.middelheimmuseum.be
Hours: July/July: 1000-2100; May/August 1000-2000; April/September 1000-1900; October-March: 1000-1700
The park is closed every Monday.

If you are looking for a nice place to relax, or you love viewing sculpture, the Middelheim Museum is perfect for you.

This grand park is home to more than 300 sculptures by Belgium's greatest artists and some of the greatest sculptors in the world. You can see pieces by Auguste Rodin, Rik Wouters, Raymond Duchamp-Villon, Henry Moore, Ossip Zadkine, and more.

The park was made into the museum in the 1950s, when Mayor Lode Craeybeckx wanted to ensure that the land was being used by the city and not being sold into smaller lots. Besides the beautiful statues, the park and its gardens also make for picturesque views.

Antwerp Zoo (Dierentuin)

Koningin Astridplein 26
Tel: 03 202 45 40
www.zooantwerpen.be

Established in July 1843, the Antwerp Zoo is one of the oldest zoos in the world, and is the oldest animal park in Belgium. Since 1843, the zoo has grown to be almost ten times its original size, now housing around 7000 animals in 950 species.

Originally, the zoo was created to encourage wildlife conservation. After World War II, it became an educational venue, and many upgrades have been made to the park since. Today, it is one of the leading zoos when it comes to scientific research and education. Surprisingly, the zoo is also a draw for those who have an eye for architecture, with many grand buildings around the complex.

Some of the most popular exhibits in the zoo include Freezeland which houses penguins and Alaskan sea otters. The Sea Lion Theatre is home to the California sea lions. Nocturama is where night active animals like the aardvark, bats, and the Senegal galago live and the Egyptian temple is where you can see Asian elephants and Baringo giraffes. This is just the tip of the iceberg when it comes to the amazing animals you will see at the zoo.

The zoo and its many wild animals make it the perfect place for both children and adults. Here you can see some of the grandest animals in the world without having to trek into the wild. There are also offer a variety of special animal shows.

The Antwerp Zoo is located next to Centraal Station and very close to Aquatopia. It is possible to buy a combined pass with Aquatopia, which helps reduce the cost of admission to both places. This combination makes these two locations the perfect way to spend a day together as a family.

Aquatopia

Koningin Astridplein 7
Tel: 03 205 07 50
www.aquatopia.be
Adult: €12.50/children 3-12 and seniors 60+: €8.50
(tickets can also be purchased in family packages at a
reduced rate)
Hours: Daily 1000-1800
Note: Aquatopia is closed Christmas Day

With water making up more than 70% of the planet, it is
no wonder that one of Antwerp's greatest sites is
Aquatopia. This giant aquarium is both educational
center and living museum, with seven 'worlds' of fish.
Fish live in rainforest, swamp, mangrove, coral reef,
ocean, lab, or submarine settings, each of which allow
guests to visit and explore.

Aquatopia is the perfect stop for those with young
children. Unlike your ordinary museum, children get to
get to see the different environments up close. It is
suggested that you visit during feeding hours as the fish
become extremely active during this time. There are more
than just fish to see as well. Aquatopia is also home to
numerous reptiles, such as snakes and lizards.

Getting to Aquatopia is easy. It is directly across the street
from Centraal Station, and is only one block from the
Franklin Rooseveltplaats bus station, which is the main
bus terminal in Antwerp.

Cathedral of our Lady (Onze Lieve Vrouwekathedraal)

Handschoenmarkt (Old City Centre)
Tel: 03 213 99 51
www.dekathedraal.be
Adults: €4/children under 12: free
Hours: Monday-Friday 1000-1700; Saturday 1000-1500;
Sunday 1300-1600

The Cathedral of Our Lady is one of the oldest buildings in Belgium. Construction of the building began in 1352, but it remained unfinished until 1521 (169 years later). Because the grand building took so long to complete, three different architects were used, giving it three distinct styles.

Along with being one of the oldest buildings in the city, it is also one of the tallest. At 123m high, the spire stands above many of the buildings in the vicinity. In fact, it is the tallest building for miles around, making is a focal point in the Old City Centre. The Cathedral of Our Lady is also the largest Gothic Cathedral in the Low Countries.

The Cathedral of Our Lady is also home to some of the greatest works of art in Antwerp outside the Royal Fine Arts Museum. Four of Rubens' best works are housed inside the cathedral. These pieces are the *Assumption* (1625), *Raising the Cross* (1610), *Resurrection* (1612), and *The Descent from the Cross* (1612).

Rubens' House (Rubenshuis)

Wapper 9-11 (Old City Centre)
Tel: 03 201 15 55
www.rubenshuis.be
Adult: €6/concession: €4/children: free
Hours: Tuesday-Sunday 1000-1700

While there are many places across Antwerp to view pieces by the master painter, perhaps one of the most interesting is Rubens' House. Not only did Ruben himself have a hand in building the mansion when he was 34 years old (1611), but it is also the home in which he died 29 years later.

Following Rubens' death, the building changed hands numerous times and the city acquired it in 1937. After spending a few years reconstructing pieces of the building to match Rubens' original, they opened a museum here in honor of his work.

The house is divided into two parts. In the first, guests can see the living quarters, along with the room that Rubens used as an art gallery. In this gallery there are many original paintings by the artist, and also paintings that he collected by other artists. During his time, the Rubens art gallery was considered to be the largest collection of art in the city. On the other side of the building is Rubens' art studio, where he worked on his masterpieces. The museum does a good job at showing how Rubens lived and worked in the last years of his life.

Centraal Station

Centraal Station Quarter

Around the start of the 20th Century, Belgium began expanding it's train lines to help more people to move across the country and across Europe. Centraal Station in Antwerp is the result of this expanding transportation sector. Designed by Louis Delancensene, the building is extremely large and very intricately detailed. One of the highlights of the building are its glass covered train platforms, which allow natural light in instead of having to use artificial light as most train platforms do. In 2009, *Newsweek* named it the fourth best train station in the world.

The Centraal Station is well placed, as its name suggests, in the center of the Old City. It is only a few steps to the Diamond District. However, if you are in search for a great diamond, you do not even have to leave the building as is home to some of the top jewelry designers in the world, with millions of dollars in diamonds available for purchase each day from the more than thirty different diamond shops.

One of the nicest things about Centraal Station is that you can visit it in all of its grandness in passing on your way other locations. Because it is a major metro stop, chances are that at some point you will use it to get to one of the other parts of Antwerp.

From 1998 to 2007, the station underwent an extensive renovation to accommodate high-speed trains like Thalys, HSL 4, and HSL-Zuid. This remodeling included two new tunnels built underneath the existing platforms. The addition of these new platforms now allows for the Amsterdam-Antwerp-Brussels-Paris train operated by Thalys to make stops at the station ten times each day. The Hague-Rotterdam-Roosendaal-Antwerp-Brussels Train also stops at the station eight times a day. Because they no longer have to return out of the city the same way they came in the trip time on these trains was reduced.

Main Square (Grote Markt)

Grote Markt is the main square in Antwerp, and offers many different attractions. First up is the city hall, which was built in the 16th century. In the center of the square is the Brabo Fountain, which was built in 1887 by Jef Lambaux. On the other side of the square are the Guild Houses, originally built in the 1500s and rebuilt after they were destroyed in a fire.

The square, which is actually shaped like a triangle, is home to many different small shops and restaurants. Tourists also enjoy sitting on one of the many benches and watching the people walk by. During Christmas, the square is home to the Christmas market, and is beautifully decorated with thousands of lights.

Grote Markt is located in the middle of the Old City Centre near to many of the other important sites in the city, making it well worth the visit.

Diamond District

This one square mile area is home to some of the world's best diamonds available for purchase. There are over 3,500 merchants all hoping that you will buy your next piece of jewelry from them. Each year, 54 billion dollars worth of diamonds pass through the district, making it one of the largest diamond districts in the world.

The diamond district even boasts its own bank, the Antwerp Diamond Bank. This bank specializes in providing banking to the many jewelry companies in the Diamond District.

Even if you do not have the money for the diamonds themselves, it is well worth the time passing through to look at all of the gorgeous pieces in the shop windows.

Het Steen

Near Scheldt River, Antwerp

This medieval fortress dates back to the 14th century shortly after the Viking incursions, making it the oldest building in Antwerp. From 1303 to 1827, the castle served as a prison. Unfortunately, today, much of the castle is gone due to demolition projects in the early 19th century, during which dozens of historic sites, including the city's oldest church, were destroyed to improve the trek through the canal. The part of the castle that does remain is rather small, but is still a beautiful site to see.

Today, the castle has become a museum where you can see many works of art created in the city over the years. There is also an excellent café, where you can enjoy your meal with a royal touch. An interesting thing about the castle is that it is home to a war memorial from World War II that does not honor Belgian troops, but instead is a strictly for Canadian soldiers.

Museum of Contemporary Art (Muhka)

Leuvenstraat 32
Tel: 03 260 99 99
www.muhka.be
Adults: €8/under 26, over 60, groups: €4/children under 13: free
Hours: Tuesday, Wednesday, Friday, Saturday, Sunday 1100-1800; Thursday 1100-2100

If you are more of a fan of modern art that of Rubens, Muhka is a must see attraction. The museum itself is a renovated grain silo and warehouse building, located in the 't Zuid area of Antwerp. The main focus of the museum is to showcase artists from Belgium and abroad. Unlike the most of the other museums in town, these collections only feature works created after the 1970s.

A nice aspect of the modern museum is that many of its artists are still alive, meaning that newer, grander pieces are coming in constantly. Attending the Museum of Contemporary Art is important if you also attend the Royal Museum of Fine Arts so you can see just how much art has changed over time, and to see how differently artists see the world today than they did in 1600.

Saint Paul's Church (Saint-Pauluskerk)

Veemarkt 14, Antwerp
http://www.mkaweb.be/site/english/026.html

Built from 1530 to 1571, Saint Paul's Church was built on top of the original, which was built in 1276. This grand church today is renowned for its collection of paintings and sculptures. It is home to three Rubens, and also includes works by Van Dyck and Jordaens. It also is home to more than 200 statues from the 17th and 18th centuries.

In 1968, a fire nearly destroyed the building, as they had in 1679. However, today, it has been completely rebuilt in all of its glory, with its artworks and sculptures having been saved by ordinary citizens worried about losing the historical pieces. A nice bonus is that the church provides guided tours, meaning someone will actually tell you about the many masterpieces that you will be looking at. These tours are available in English, French, and Dutch.

FotoMuseum

Waalsekaai 47, Antwerp
Tel: +32 3 242 93 00
www.fotomuseum.be
Adults: €7/youth under 26: €1/children under 12: free
Hours: Tuesday-Sunday 1000-1800

If you are a fan of great photography, the FotoMuseum is

the museum for you. Opened in 2004, the museum has thousands of photos on display, along with cameras and other tools used by photographers since its inception in the 19th century. The FotoMuseum features photographers from around the world, and not just Belgium, making it more of an international museum instead of just a local one. FotoMuseum is more than just an art gallery, as it holds things like family albums, business photography, printed texts with photographs, and more.

Recommendations for the Budget Traveller

Places to Stay

Antwerp City Center Hotel

Appelmansstraat 31, Antwerp
Tel: +32 3 203 54 00

Located in the Diamond District, this hotel is in the
perfect area for those who want to be in the center of it all.

Grote Market, Rubens House, and Central Station are all within walking distance. There is also a tram stop only 300 m from the entrance.

All rooms include a television, telephone, wireless internet, a safe, and a hair dryer. The hotel also offers laundry facilities, a left-luggage office, and a safety deposit box. Breakfast is an additional cost of €12.50 per person. There is also no parking at the hotel, but public parking is only 10m away. Rooms start out around €37.00 per night, with children under 3 free.

Hotel Postiljon

Blauwmoezelstraat 6, Antwerp
Tel: +32 3 231 75 75
www.hotelpostiljon.be

The Hotel Postiljon is located within a short distance from the Cathedral of Our Lady and the Grote Markt. Groenplaats metro station is only 300m away, as are tram lines 10 and 11. This hotel offers 21 rooms, available in only double or quadruple rooms. Some rooms have private baths, while some rooms only have sinks, and must share their bathrooms with others.

Every room comes with a television, Wi-Fi, and heating. Suites also offer mini-bars. At the 24 hour reception area, guests also have access to a safety deposit box, a TV lounge, and luggage storage. There is private parking available at the hotel, but you must pay a fee in order to use it. Breakfast is also available, at an additional charge of €11.00 per person.

Boomerang Hostel

Lange Leemstraat 95, 2018, Antwerp
Tel: +32 3 238 47 82
www.boomeranghostel.be

Located at only 10 minutes walk from the city center, the Boomerang Hostel is perfect for those with a lower budget. The four-storey building offers dorm style living in either female-only or mixed gender rooms.

The hostel provides access to a kitchen, baggage storage, Wi-Fi, and 24/7 access to communal showers. Sheets are available for €2.50, as is breakfast in the morning. Beds in the hostel start out at only €12, making it perfect if you'd rather be spending your money on food and diamonds.

Abhostel

Kattenberg 110, Antwerp
Tel: +32 473 57 01 66
www.abhostel.com

Converted from an old chocolate factory, this hostel comes with everything you need. There is a fully equipped kitchen, a bar, a DVD corner, Wi-Fi, sheets, and lockers. Plus, there is no lockout like many other hostels, meaning you can come and go as you please without having to worry about whether or not someone will be at the desk to beep you in.

You must be sure to list your arrival time when you expect to first check into the hostel when you book as the owners are not always in the building. Otherwise, normal check-in is from 1300-1500 and 1800-2000. This hostel offers twin rooms, a five bed mixed dorm, and a twelve bed mixed dorm, all of which have shared bathrooms.

This hostel has an age restriction of 50 years old and younger.

Condo Gardens Antwerp Studios

De Pretstraat 11, Antwerp
Tel: +32 473 44 09 15
www.be-housing.be

Located slightly further from the city centre, these apartments offer a unique way to stay in Antwerp. There are 56 units in the building, available in studio, family rooms, or apartments suited for 2, 3, or 4 people. Each unit comes with its own bathroom, a fully equipped kitchen with microwave and fridge, a television, and Wi-Fi. The building is also pet friendly, at an additional fee.

As stated, the Condo Gardens are nearly a twenty minutes walk from the Cathedral of Our Lady. It is also near the Diamond District, which is about 15 minutes away. The closest public transportation is roughly 500m away from the building.

Places to Eat & Drink

Wijnbar Vigneto

Wijngaardstraat 5, Antwerp 2000
Tel: +32 33459565
www.wijnbar.nl

Whether you are a professional wine connoisseur, or just enjoy the occasional glass, Wijnbar is the perfect place to grab a drink at a reasonable price, with wines in available in every price range. Wines are available from many different countries around the world, giving you the option to try the many different flavors different areas around the globe create. There is also a wide selection of tapas type dishes available to have with your drink. The customer service at the bar is also highly praised.

Bart-A-Vin

Lange Slachterijstraat 3-5, Antwerp 2060
Tel: +32 474 94 17 86
www.bartavin.info

Based on French cuisine, this bar features exquisite wine couple with even more exquisite food. While the wine menu is extensive, the food menu is relatively small.

This is because the owners wish to focus more on fresh product and good food than a large quantity of food available. A unique aspect of the bar is that there is no wine list. Although there are 200 different wines from around Europe, you do not get the opportunity to pick one out yourself. Instead, you talk with Bart, the main bartender, about your preferences, and he brings you out the wine that he believes will be perfect for you.

Eten Vol Leven

Minderbroedersrui 52, Antwerp
Tel: 03 232 33 34 64
http://www.etenvolleven.be/

If you are looking for a unique restaurant in Antwerp, this is just the place for you. This restaurant is one hundred percent vegan, and also offers some interesting raw foods. They carry salads, soups, wraps, and desserts, and also occasionally have specialties like pizza or zucchini-spaghetti. They are also well known for their fresh juices and smoothies. Once a month, they remain open for a four-course dinner of their specialty foods.

Another unique aspect of eten vol leven is that it offers a workshop on cooking with all natural ingredients. These workshops are available in French, English, and Spanish, giving every visitor the opportunity to create and enjoy their wonder foods.

't Koekebakske

Leeuwemnstraat 23, Antwerp 2000
Tel: +32 494 07 17 77

On your way to the Plantin-Moretus Museum, be sure to stop by this amazing restaurant for a hearty breakfast to get you through the day. This bistro offers one of the best Belgian breakfasts in Antwerp in a small, cozy location. They even offer British and American favorites like bacon and eggs or pancakes. The bistro is well worth the price for the portions served.

Amadeus

St-Paulusplaats 20, Antwerp 2000
Tel: 03 232 25 87
www.amadeusspareribrestaurant.be

If you are looking to try some great Belgian food, Amadeus is the place to go. They are most known for their amazing racks of ribs, which are all you can eat, coupled with numerous Belgian beers available. Amadeus is located near Grote Markt, making it the perfect way to end a day of shopping and site seeing in the city.

The restaurant is also great at accommodating families with children. However, their specialty is accommodating the large groups that many other restaurants are unwilling or unable to work with. No matter how many people you will be having at dinner, though, it is best to make a reservation ahead of time to ensure a spot.

Reload

Korte Winkelstraat 11, Antwerp
Tel: 0475 96 42 84
www.reloadantwerpen.be
Hours: Lunch 1200-1400; Dinner 1800-2130

If great food and service is what you look for in a restaurant, Reload is the place to go. Their Belgian cuisine comes in generous portions, and won't break the bank. Because Reload is so popular, it is important that you book your table ahead of time, or they might not be able to accommodate you otherwise.

Reload offers daily specials along with their normal menu. But, these are not your normal daily specials. Instead, they are specialty foods such as horse steak or rabbit. For the beer connoisseurs, it is important to note that there are no beers on tap, and that everything comes in bottles.

Frituur No 1

Hoogstraat 1 (Old City Centre), Antwerp
Hours: Monday-Sunday 1100-2200

Belgium is known for their fascination with *frites* which is similar to a French fry. Frituur is considered the best place in Antwerp to get these delectably fried potatoes at a low cost.

They do have other food available, but most people go for the fries with a side of meat instead of the other way around like usual. The restaurant only serves local cuisine, such as Flemish stew with fries, all of which are available for cheap.

A unique aspect of Frituur is its design. To order, you walk up to a counter stall that opens up to the street. Once you receive your food, you can either choose to find someplace else to eat it, or you can go next door to their dining area. The choice is yours, and makes this restaurant different from many of the others around town.

Places to Shop

Chinatown Antwerp

The Antwerp Chinatown is the only one in Belgium. Like its counterparts in other cities it provides many different gift shops, specialty shops, and grocery stores that have lots of items on sale at relatively low prices. It is conveniently located near Centraal Station and the Antwerp Zoo.

RA Christmas Market

Ra, Kloosterstraat 13, Antwerp 2000

If you happen to be in Antwerp between November 26th and December 25th, the Christmas Market is the perfect place to buy many different types of trinkets. You can find sculptures, knitwear, handcrafted Christmas décor, secondhand objects and more, all for a great price. The market is open Wednesday to Saturday 1100 to 1900, and Sunday 1100 to 1800.

Bazar Bizar

Steenhouwersvest 18, Antwerp

If you are looking for items that are a bit more exotic than northwest European try Bazar Bizar. This shop sells lots of exotic furniture, jewelry, accessories, and more, all which seem to have been pulled directly out of Aladdin. The shop also has a bed and breakfast upstairs, which makes it another great option for cheap living.

Vogelenmarkt (Birds Market)

Oudevaartplaats, Theaterplein, and surrounding area
Hours: Sunday 800 to 1300

This weekly market is open year-round and here you can buy goods at a decent price.

This market sells everything thing from animals (hamsters, rabbits, birds, etc), to fabrics, flowers, antiques and more. With all of the things for sale at the market there is sure to be something for everyone here.

Stadsfeestzaal

Hopland 21, Meir, Antwerp
Tel: 03 202 31 00
www.stadsfeestzaal.com

Originally built in 1908, this grand building today has become one of the best shopping centers in Antwerp. In 2000, the building burnt completely to the ground. Because it was listed as a protected monument it was rebuilt exactly as before. Many people recommend stopping by Stadsfeestzaal, which is near Centraal Station, even if you do not particularly care to shop just enjoy the amazing architecture. Today, the mall has forty different shops with items for everyone.

Labels

Aalmoezenierstraat 4, Antwerp
www.labelsinc.be

Designer clothing can often be expensive, but at Labels, you can get some of the top designers for low, affordable costs. Whether you are looking for shoes, clothing, or accessories, Labels has it all for both men and women.

Labels is conveniently located between the City Centre and the City Hall.

Printed in Great Britain
by Amazon.co.uk, Ltd.,
Marston Gate.